WHETHER THE WEATHER

A collection of poems

RUHEEN KUMAR

Copyright © 2023 by Ruheen Kumar

All rights reserved. This book or any portion thereof may not be reproduced or used in any manner whatsoever without the express written permission of the publisher except for the use of brief quotations in a book review or scholarly journal.

First Printing: 2023

ISBN 9798373438636

to
my mom and Tani

WHETHER the WEATHER

whether the weather
is fine
or not
don't let the petals
rise
why not
let them crinkle and die
watch them
curl up
cover their insides
darken around
the edges
hang on for their lives
whether the weather
pulls them up
or not
don't
walk
outside
and give them love
even beautiful things
should feel
the torment
of neglect
or else how will they
learn
to be
whether the weather
is fine
I wish you could tell us
it's alright

Space

there is an empty space
i'm just not sure I'm allowed to take it

i will stare at it wondering
then turn away hesitant

when i finally gain the courage
someone will have taken my place

Clothes

if the clothes hanging in my closet
start getting bigger
i know
i'm either eating too much
or hiding under sweaters

if they all turn from black to white
i feel like I'm asking for attention
i look in the mirror
and force my smile away
"don't get ahead of yourself
you're losing direction"

i need to feel bad about myself
to get the right motivation
hide under sweaters
that shield me from affection

camouflage

Can you pretend not
To love me today?
So I can fulfill my
Fantasy of being
Unloved and isolated?
And pretend to
Be the archetype
Of underappreciated?
So just for today
And then I hope you
Go back to loving me
Again.

Nail

if i get closer
i get scared
that i don't mean
what i say
instead
i pick on the skin
around
my nails.

Maria

the effect of a good story

In the dim light of a flame
You start imagining traces of smiles
On your partner's face
Only to realise you're merely
Indulging in the pretense
Satisfying your morbid, cruel curiosity
In the name of love
Because you know you will
Abandoned regardless
In more ways than one

Fire

when you light a match
watch the flame
burn it black
wisps of smoke
reach your fingers
it's warm
it's exciting
then you put it out
it's still warm
part of it
permanently black
vulnerable
so you let it
crumble

i'm sure there's a metaphor in there somewhere

late hours of the night
palms open by the candlelight
tension simmers
in the corner
of my eye
passion or love and
aggression
an ember sparks
in my mind

let the heat consume me
whisper in the slightest
of voices
'how wistful was i?'
how fickle, simple
disillusioned
as time
spun the wheels
in unkind directions
with feelings and
complications

l

i

g

h

t

candle

i let my palm hover
too close
to the fire and its
warmth
feel the burn travelling
across the treacherous
waters
of hindsight

and out the window
the cardinals
are vying for a place
to be hypnotized
near the candlelight

l
i
g
h
t

bathroom

we're not afraid of the dark
it's not all that scary
we're afraid of the unfamiliarity of the dark
the fact that there may be something in it
and we don't know
we're not used to it
but when you're alone
in a place you know like the back of your hand
and your eyes adjust to the darkness
it's actually quite peaceful
the dark
you can see everything clearly

and then someone turns the light on

Reaction

You're at a point
Where you don't know
If you're the reflection
Or the person
Standing upright

You're left with
The same bitter taste
Of a thousand misfortunes
Mistakes and delusions
And regrets you wish you made

in *your* eyes

Under starlight
The moon shines
With faded affection
For the overwhelming sky
Touch dissipates
And your fingers, they shake
As they reminisce and realize
That you
Were lonely
If lonely was the chaos
In your eyes

A different kind of hell

if only we could exist
for a single moment
at only one place
for only a memory
that would be solely ours

but we are flesh and blood
we travel and continue
to exist at different times
in different places
we cannot seem to stop
yet we believe
our existence
is extraordinary

when will we realise
that even the extraordinary
is ordinary?

A *cherry* for your thoughts

cherry-picked words
taste sweeter on
my tongue
than your hand-picked
cherries

blood *moon*

I look up at the sky,
Between the trees
An iridescent glow
The moon peeks
Out from behind
The hill that hides
Whether the moon
Is pushed
Or pulls itself up
And chooses to reveal
It's reds and yellows
Only to kindness:
Those beside me
I can't see the moon
Through the leaves
Here I am believing
In my misfortune
While they appreciate
The light the moon
Shares impartially
Unabashed, unafraid

I need a change
In my perspective
Reach out to shift
The leaves
Turn my head left
Maybe I can see
The sunlight given
To the moon
To use as its own
The creator is easily
Forgotten
When the performer
Is all they can see
Maybe they should
Change where they sit
The blood moon
Is only blood
When the sun gives too
much.

Hungry

I cannot breathe
I should not be allowed to speak
So I dig my fingernails into my neck
And rip out my throat
Dragging my lungs along
I'll hang them up on a wall
Bloody flesh dripping red
But my hands tear my skin
Forgetting to be delicate
So I use the hammer to crush
The bones in my fingers
I'll hang these up too
Limp hands that rattle as they shake
My legs take me in untoward
Directions to people
Instead of the wall
So I saw them off myself
Sculpting the edges
To be round and raw
I'll hang one on either end

Now the wall just looks incomplete
I peel the ears off my head
Gouge the eyes from my skull
Shave the tip of my nose
Slice my brain into two
Force my mouth to curve upwards
At last, for my centerpiece,
The main attraction
The sensibility behind this exhibit
My heart
Nailed to the wall
Scarlet, pulsing within a frame
Gorgeous and grotesque
I am on the floor
Writhing in pain
I gaze at my reminders,
My final pieces of artwork
The stomach remains

Even as I'm left in shambles
There is still much to take
You remain insatiable
Hungry.

lyricism

i lack the lyricism
they all expect
me to have when
i'm feeling miserable
and can't confess
with my tongue
but instead
have to express
in writing
because it's best
to have an outlet

so you don't
regress
into patterns
you thought
you left and
disregard the
feelings you
expelled
because they
haven't disappeared
and are merely
suppressed
and then i
ask myself

"what the hell am i doing?"

my urge to pop a
child's
balloon
and watch them cry
as i laugh
is
overwhelming

it's on par with my urge
to shove
a knife in my throat
just to
see
what happens

how morbid. i know

but aren't we all?

intrusive

Train to Paris

I remember the inside:
A little red; a bit of grey.
Rows of leather seats and carpeted floors.
But it was when the journey began,
And I sat down,
My feet dangling over the edge,
Just like my anticipation -
They told me we'll be under the sea.
But I felt us moving;
The slow hum I heard eased me.
My eyes flickered to the window,
My parents' voices faded,
As I watched my reflection.
Then I noticed her. In the window.
I recognized her,
From where we had left.
It was while I was on my feet,
Hand clasped in my mother's,
But eyes fixed on her.
The girl sat waiting, sketchbook in her lap,
Pencil in her hand with her legs crossed.
It was crowded and clamorous,
Yet she paid no attention,
Her gaze set on her art,
Her movements steady.
The girl's raven hair was tied
And I think she wore something blue.

We went in together.
We sat on the left,
She sat on the right,
And drew.
And drew.
And drew.
And her pencil left dark marks on off-white paper,
As her hands moved fast, then slow.
I couldn't help but watch.
I strained to look away,
But the window only showed
Black bricks.
Darker than her hair. And her pencil.
We were underwater, but I didn't care.
I was more intrigued by the girl
Who sat so close, but was so far away.
Living in a different world.
I was helpless, shy, way too curious.
I wondered what she was thinking. And drawing.
It was pure, innocent fascination.
Then the train stopped.
She stopped.
I stopped.
Because we had arrived.
We left.
She was gone.
I was bored.
Again.

cherry Blossoms

The old man dragged his sickle across
The roots of his wheat harvest
He swept his brow of dirt and sweat
And collected the pieces of earth
To place into his wheelbarrow;
His companion, eternally loyal
Yet vulnerable to the curse of time

The old man pulled his friend
Through lifeless thickets of people
Before deciding to push him
As if he were leading at the hull
Of a ship tearing through waters
But the Red Sea would not part
So he had to kick with his own legs

The old man travelled forward
Even when the wheels caught
In the gravel, in the sand
In the animal tracks of machines
He shivered as his vision tinted blue
The hand he held begged him
Never to let go

cherry Blossoms

The old man nudged his friend
Through distinct seasons alike
Around him, flowers bloomed
Bursting with a life he once had
His grip thawed as his friend
Pushed faster to see the buds
Bend their necks backwards

The old man ambled further
His naked chest gleamed
With droplets of perspiration
That curled up on his thin hairs
The sun pried open the skies
Mercilessly and his friend scorched
His hand, forcing him away

The wheelbarrow sped far
Into a land where flowers died
The world was on fire
But words praised the beauty
Of rosy cherry blossoms
That were taken or had fallen
Only to be forgotten until next time

cherry Blossoms

The old man chased his friend
His strides long and slow; experienced
His friend stopped, pausing because
In the slew of death remained
A single pink cherry blossom
The old man picked up the flower
And urged his friend along the path

He crumpled the cherry blossom in his hand
For he did not need a friend that would vanish
Behind him, the trees shook their heads
As he walked, cherry blossoms embraced
The old man and his wheelbarrow

He smiled and went on his way
The sakura followed gladly
"Until next time." They said.

a cup of coffee

conversations over the counter
no one's trying to be discreet

a boy and a girl in the corner
man and woman behind me

one just fell in love
the other was blinded

another was burned
too much excitement

pages turn with sighs
ice melts and steam rises

some tell slanted truths and lies
situations are romanticized

the machine gets louder
people get jittery

oh, the things that can happen over
a cup of coffee

Water

It's easy to start making up your own stories. Fabricating your memories in ways that you wished they had played out. Manipulating words because language is superficial. Changing meanings because change is constant. The memories in your mind are a like movie. You're just editing the script.

When you're in the water, monsters tend to surface when it's silent. They catch you off guard. It happens when you're alone. Floating in the middle of nowhere.

Words you wished you'd never said. Hands you wished you'd never let go of. Colors you wished you'd never seen. They rise to the surface, ready to consume you whole. Open mouth, baring their razor-like fangs as they hiss, slithering towards you. They swallow you whole, their fangs piercing deep into your bones, leaving hollow marks that can never be fully refilled.

Because not all monstrous things appear as monsters.

And then your eyes open. You're drowning in a blue abyss, so you push yourself up until you can see your feet peek out of the water. The world's filter has changed; everything is grey now.

The cold bites at your toes, a chill settling into your bones. An incessant ache. A permanent reminder that you lost your skin.

Even if it regrows - you already let the monsters in.

> the water can be a dangerous place